GIOTTO

ABOUT THE AUTHOR

Dr. Camillo Semenzato is a professor at the University of Padua. He is Editor of the magazine *Arte Veneta* and his published writings include many articles on mediaeval and contemporary art, and also, of particular distinction, on the sculpture of the sixteenth, seventeenth and eighteenth centuries.

DR. CAMILLO SEMENZATO

Giotto

BARNES & NOBLE, INC.

NEW YORK

Publishers • Booksellers • Since 1873

Editor: Anthony Bosman
Lay-out: Wim van Stek
Published in the United States in 1964
by Barnes & Noble, Inc., 105 Fifth Avenue, New York 3, N.Y.
© 1964 and printed in Holland by The Ysel Press Ltd, Deventer

At the beginning of the thirteenth century there appeared the great figure who played a decisive role in the renewal of Italian culture: St. Francis. In the towns and cities a new class, the bourgeoisie, was taking shape, while the traditional religious culture of the High Middle Ages was undergoing a transformation in response to new needs. Theological dogmatism had to face continuous attack from the movements of renovation and from society's profound, though not yet fully conscious, search for new values, worldly as well as religious. Heresies and outbreaks of rebellion were springing up everywhere and the traditional authorities, the Papacy and the Church, were unable to find a point of contact between the demands of the old order and the new popular longings. Then, suddenly, appeared St. Francis, who understood the ardour and the truth of the heresies while retaining his respect for the authority of Rome. Faith was renewed around him: its age-old theological form was maintained, but fed by new, living springs of human understanding.

It is hardly necessary to remind the reader of the essence of what St. Francis preached: his exaltation of poverty, his acceptance of the world and of life—their earthly as well as their spiritual values. In the teaching of St. Francis, Christ's message of love was steeped in reality and the problems arising from ascetic theories were related to everyday life. That message of love was given new meaning for the citizens of the new industrious bourgeois society which was accelerating the end of the Middle Ages in Italy.

The teaching of St. Francis also decisively affected the literature and the art of his time, which were so closely linked with religion as to be almost identical with it.

As it approached the Renaissance, Italian culture was becoming more and more humanistic and secular; it was, in all Europe, the culture which contained the most germs of transformation. But this transformation had to proceed slowly, and could not be openly revolutionary. It was necessary for it to be sponsored by religious authority itself, and only a saint could have assumed the task of giving new values to the world and its interests, to reality and nature, to the very joy of living.

Italian society of the thirteenth century was aware of the greatness and the importance of St. Francis. In his birthplace, Assisi, there was erected in his honour a basilica, which was one of the most beautiful and one of the most imposing of an epoch in which monumental churches were springing up everywhere. It stands out not only on account of its size and its simple architectural beauty, but above all because, towards the end of the century, the greatest artists of the time worked in it — as if the greatness of the Saint had the power to attract the greatest craftsmen about his earthly remains.

Two great schools of art, the Florentine, represented by Cimabue, who was already famous, and the Roman school, headed by Jacopo Torriti, shared the work of decorating the church. In the Florentine style (and in that of Cimabue) there appeared not only the conventional and highly refined forms of Byzantine tradition but also the expressionist tendencies of Tuscan-Romanesque culture, which, originating with Giunta Pisano and passed on by Coppo di Marcovaldo, had called forth in Cimabue the sense of tragedy as well as the sense of grandeur. On the other hand, the Roman school, which had now reached a very high level of creative originality, was quick to transmit, through the balanced productions of its best representatives, such as Pietro Cavallini and Jacopo Torriti (both of whom worked at Assisi), an almost classical and pre-Renaissance sense of proportion, which had been deeply nourished on the culture of the South, had already reached Tuscany with the sculptor Nicola Pisano, and was now triumphing with absolute power in the sculptures of Arnolfo di Cambio.

It is at this decisive moment of fateful encounters, and in this church sacred to the memory of the greatest Italian saint, that for the first time we meet Giotto.

It is probable that he had painted before coming to Assisi. According to the old documents, Giotto was born in 1266, at Vespignano in the Mugello or in Florence, but nothing is known about his youth, there are only legends. The only facts are those of his artistic beginnings in Assisi, but even these are unclear and difficult to establish. The artist was still young, and only gradually, as his style matured, did he inspire respect among his companions in the workshop.

At one time the critics attributed to Giotto only those illustrations of the life of St. Francis painted by him and his followers between 1296 and 1299. Today, daring to go further back, we see his hand in the great "Stories of the Old and New Testaments", which began in the arms of the transept and were completed gradually by Cimabue's workshop. In these frescoes it is possible to detect, at first only in details, the hand of a new master whose work is leading to very high summits; it is increasingly distinguished, as regards form, by a new plasticity and monumentality, and spiritually by extreme clarity of thought and a search for living humanity. This master, who stands out more and more from the other anonymous followers of Cimabue, can perhaps be glimpsed for the first time in "Jesus on the Way to Calvary", appears more clearly in "The Deposition" and is triumphantly manifest in "The Story of Isaac". In these pictures Giotto's language has already acquired

7

its fundamental components, and although he was still capable of immense potential development (which is very exceptional in a mediaeval painter), here he was already establishing the permanent bases of his art.

What Giotto seems to be mainly seeking is plasticity of form. The revolutionary character of Giotto's painting, his concreteness, which is absolutely new in comparison with that feeling for the abstract and incorporeal which had characterized the former neo-Hellenistic tradition, is all there. It is true that Giunta Pisano, Coppo and other masters had already rejected the traditional two-dimensionality of mediaeval and Byzantine painting and that Romanesque culture in Italy had already tended to emphasize the plasticity of the body, but it is also true that up to this time, in painting, this movement consisted of attempts accompanied by continual compromises and that the emergence of form was opposed by the use of line and colour in a desperate attempt to construct, above the clear outlines of the relief, the dizzy reaches of abstract space.

No master had ever before so consciously attempted such a spectacular emergence of form, or created such an impressive volume, which through the striking representation of depth has a sense of grandeur. This is enhanced by the isolation of the figures and the simplification of their gestures.

In these compositions every form has a very definite and essential function which makes all further description, symbolism or comment, superfluous. Mediaeval art, striving to exalt supernatural truths, was not only inclined towards signs and symbols, but very often, even in masters now described as "primitives", also tried to attain a great richness of attributes and of courtly and ornamental language. But Giotto was extremely simple, even austere; he sought neither elegance nor preciosity nor superfluity, but always kept to what was essential. His language derived its nobility and power from its own truth, which was founded on the effort to attain complete clarity. He trusted entirely in the intrinsic force of what he had to say and the long pauses that accompanied his statements. His lofty discourse is slow, marked by the silences which give sonorous immensity to every affirmation. It is weighty, calm and rational. This rationalism of Giotto's springs from that sense of measure, that clear proportion and compositional balance, which keep his paintings free from irrelevant description and also from effusions of irrationality. His sense of measure, which is also his classicality, is the sign of a watchful conscience which never loses control over itself and which, in a state of enthusiasm or anguish, does not lose sight of the deep significance of every event. Joy and suffering can only sharpen his vision, not overthrow it; they can never tear it away from its logical roots, from the clarity of mind which with serene sagacity guards the depth of his soul and which in creating a form can always give a precise logical meaning to an apparently random movement or an apparently unreal occurrence.

That is why Giotto's painting is so luminously clear. The relief of the forms is powerful, the drawing is decisive, but the luminous colours are so sensitive that they produce extremely delicate effects. This sensitivity, so obvious and yet so subtle, is another element of Giotto's style, one which enables him to give the most human nuances to his language.

These, then, are the principal components of Giotto's art; they were still in a germinal state, still enclosed in a rind of traditional decorum, like a powerful energy which has found only a small outlet.

Giotto had already possessed himself of the narrative power of Cimabue, who harmonized his forms by means of his typical monumentality, but he had also experimented with, and made his own, the plastic clarity of Arnolfo di Cambio, who in Rome, Perugia and Orvieto led the radiant classicism of Nicola Pisano

9

to a new sense of measure, a new synthesis, a new and more architectonic sense of balance.

These acute and genial interpretations of the culture of his time seem to us possible with Giotto because his attitude toward the traditional Byzantinesque art had undergone a profound change, and this brings us back to the key figure of our whole discussion: St. Francis. Giotto's passion for reality and simplicity, his courage to love concrete things, all seem to us to be confirmed in St. Francis. Giotto was the child of that great moment in history, and no one but he could have told the story of the great Saint on the walls of the church in Assisi.

Between the frescoes of Isaac and St. Francis we find such a great advance of maturity that we must assume an interval of some years and regard as more than probable a journey by the painter to Rome. Giotto could already have learned the characteristics of the Roman school at Assisi from Torriti, but at Rome he could not only see the works of Torriti and Arnolfo, but also those of Cavallini. Rome meant for him the confirmation of his classicism. The special qualities of Cavallini's painting are mostly those of rhythm and of a grand and solemn courtliness. Cavallini's chromatic subtlety must also have attracted Giotto (who at Assisi had come in contact with Cimabue's violent expressionism) and led him to modulate his colour towards tints which could express the most delicate impulses of his sensibility and which offered him new expressive possibilities, particularly in a more naturalistic way. Moreover, in Rome Giotto saw Arnolfo at the height of his activity, and could admire the decorated architecture of the Cosmati, reminiscences of which are preserved in the Padua frescoes. At least until his later work in Padua, Giotto's cultural experience may be said to have concluded with these contacts.

The first scene of "The History of St. Francis" painted by Giotto

10

at Assisi is the one where the Saint gives his cloak to a beggar (p. 21). The episode takes place outside the town, in the deep peace of the country. The horse grazing at the left repeats the rhythmic curves of the mountains and emphasizes this peace by bringing it up to the foreground; the only movement to interrupt it is that of St. Francis offering his cloak. The profiles of the mountains converge towards him; we feel that he, in the geometric centre of the scene, is not only its chief character but remains isolated, not really being a part of either of the two compositional systems to his right and left; it is as if he substantially does not belong to any earthly locality.

In this, as in other pictures, St. Francis is placed deliberately in natural surroundings which are remarkable for their grandeur. The action in these scenes is less fluid than in the later frescoes painted at Padua, because the rhythms are less fused and the gestures are more incisive. Every time Giotto depicts a figure or an action, there is such tension in the vigorous plasticity that the figures seem to break through their two-dimensionality and to push against the static surfaces which tend to circumscribe their movements. It seems as if Giotto always had to struggle against this inert spatial shell, and did so with great energy, striking great blows against it — like a sculptor hammering his chisel, we might say, in view of the architectonic solidity of his forms.

From this was derived a movement which may have been slow, or heavy, but was always imposing, with that strength which Roman expressionism could always put into its almost symbolic gestures.

Among the most intense of these plastic episodes is the "Dream of Pope Innocent III" (pp. 22, 23), in which the precariously balanced building supported by the Saint weighs like a nightmare over the sleeping Pontiff. In each of these scenes there is the endeavour to create space, to empty out the formless mediaeval "fullness", so that the figures can have room to develop their actions freely. In some scenes this effort attains particular compositional vigour, as in the picture of "Innocent III Approving the Rule" (p. 24), where the power of the architectural relief is clearly developed in depth, and is not inferior to that of the figures. It is all very crowded, as if to suggest some ceremony to solemnize a decree, and the rhythm has something lively and triumphant in it.

Giotto did not care about exact realistic relations between the figures and the architectural space in which they are placed; often this space is merely symbolic, as with the town of Arezzo in the scene of the Saint driving out the demons (p. 27). Only the church which rises majestically to the left has some proportional relation with the praying Saint and the friar holding up the cross (which is no longer visible). But even in this case the grandeur is largely symbolic and is intended to give concreteness to the moral value of the Saint humbly kneeling and praying. The immense church symbolizes the great force which he is emitting.

Opposite the church is the town from which the demons are fleeing. It is a symbolic town, of unreal proportions, but the houses and towers heaped up inside the walls are extremely concrete. In other scenes such landscape descriptions are merely commentary on the central action, but here the town plays the chief part.

There is certainly no realistic perspective, but instead we have the true atmosphere of a mediaeval town, such as we can still find in the Apennines, with jutting corners, deep, narrow streets, invisible alleys, overhanging walls; a chessboard, a labyrinth, but with glorious façades and balconies upon the tops of the stratified buildings.

The absorbed prayer of the Saint and the forceful gesture of the friar cause the devils to flee in panic, and behind them the city

12

shines out, liberated, clean, purified. The demons fly off as if catapulted by an explosion; they shoot up over the steeples, they find no room for their flight, even in the sky, which rejects them and forces them to escape through a narrow passage.

In this fresco, as in many others, Giotto has isolated the Saint from the centre of action, almost as if he wanted to express the sense of his meditation and of his not belonging to this world. In "The Miracle of the Spring" (p. 28) St. Francis is so deep in prayer that he does not seem to notice that his prayer has already been granted. The rhythmical play of lines inserts his figure into the naked, austere mountain's great rocky surfaces, which make the bursting forth of the water appear all the more miraculous. As in other scenes, the figures of the friars do not directly take part in the episode. The opening of the sky, which comes down between the mountains, as far as the head of St. Francis, isolates the two friars on the left and their only function is to provide a commentary.

The friars in the Franciscan scenes are like a chorus; they are nearly always passive spectators, surprised at the miracle; their limited and contingent interest enhances, by contrast, the profundity and sublime significance of every one of the Saint's actions.

Similarly profound is "The Sermon to the Birds" (p. 29), one of the most beautiful pictures of the entire series.

In this fresco we find the most lush, the most vernal trees ever painted by Giotto; their foliage seems to point to the infinite spaces of the air; the horizon is lowered almost to the bottom of the picture, in order to increase the vastness of the blue sky. The foliage, the birds, and the Saint frame an open space in which a bird, flying down with open wings, becomes the pivot of the scene. This open space permits direct communication between the Saint and the little creatures; one hand of St.

13

Francis seems to be held out towards the bird just descending, the other towards those perched on the ground.

Among the last of the frescoes of the Assisi cycle in which Giotto's work is apparent (the last were finished by very close pupils) is the dramatic scene of the "Death of the Knight of Celano" (p. 31), which is also one of the most complex.

Here once again the moral solitude of St. Francis is stressed by various elements: he stands higher than all the other figures and he is framed by the large architectural forms. In the part of the picture where the Saint stands, everything is profoundly motionless and orderly. Only the table, which is set for a meal and is painted in a lively and naturalistic manner, corresponds with the narrative manner of the other part of the picture, where figures crowd around the dead Knight. There is surprise and anguish here, but in spite of its tragedy it is a mere chronicled event, the significance of which does not extend beyond the agitation of the individuals. The sense of the supernatural comes from the immobility of St. Francis and from his look, which falls directly on the dead Knight, passing over the dismay of the others.

Although few traces of his activities there remain, we know that Giotto was called to Rome about 1300 to paint for the Jubilee. Among his pre-Paduan work, the painted crucifix (p. 20), a youthful work in the church of Santa Maria Novella, in Florence, can be ascribed to him with certainty. But the next great phase of his activity came at Padua.

We do not know for certain when Giotto painted the frescoes in the Scrovegni Chapel (often called the Arena Chapel) in Padua. All we know is that the chapel (the architecture of which has been attributed to Giotto) was begun in 1303 and that it was consecrated in 1305, but we have no confirmation that the paintings were finished at the time of the consecration. However, the majority of scholars date the painting of the frescoes to around these years. Giotto had already painted in Padua previously, and was to paint there later, but nothing more of his work has survived, just as nothing of his has remained at Rimini, Verona, Bologna, Milan, Naples and other places where we know he probably worked.

It is possible that Enrico Scrovegni, the Paduan nobleman who commissioned the work, had known Giotto at Padua. The chapel was part of his palace, which stood within the ancient Roman amphitheatre (hence "Arena Chapel") and which was demolished in the last century.

The frescoes of the chapel are spread out in three bands. The topmost tells the stories of the Virgin, and the two lower, the stories of Christ. Below these (in niches of the plinth) are monochrome allegorical paintings of the Virtues and Vices. On the entrance wall is a Last Judgement. Some medallions decorate the barrel-vaulted ceiling, upon which the vault of heaven is painted. There are other frescoes in the small apse, but these are of a later date.

Giotto's work in Padua shows notable development in comparison with the Assisi frescoes. At Assisi he had already attained great clarity of composition; but he achieved a new and even more measured balance in the Padua frescoes. In the ones at Assisi the parts of a scene, though in relation with each other, remain separate, as if the effect Giotto wanted to achieve came rather from the force of the details than from the unity of the whole.

In Padua the component parts of a scene are nearly always easily subordinated to the general scheme. The space in which the action takes place is much more united, the action itself flows with a more open movement, and has lost the viscous character of the Assisi paintings. The expressionistic tension of lines and volumes attains better balance by means of more measured correlation between the parts. In Assisi many figures and many events were crowded into one picture, but at Padua every detail is clearly subordinated to the main action, which plays the principal part in the picture.

As regards form, his feeling for space reached a greater and more "classical" coherence in Padua. At Assisi Giotto already possessed the feeling for monumental space conceived with imposing proportions through almost motionless volumes. In Padua the internal relations of this space were more thoroughly examined with regard to the possibilities it afforded for movement, and any feeling of grandeur and impressiveness that was lost was made up for by gains in feeling for measure and logic. But there always remained a monumental space.

Here it will be well to say a little more about Giotto's space, because it is so important for understanding his art. Giotto knew no perspective in the Renaissance meaning of the term because he did not possess the notion of the infinite. At a certain point his scene closes and he comes up against the abstract limits of mediaeval tradition. But before closing this limited space, which is perhaps suggestive of the space on the stage of a mystery play, he articulated it with such coherence and precision, with such graduation of relationships, that it is in no way inferior to that of the Florentine Renaissance — in fact, it is its clear predecessor. It is a logical space, represented in accordance with a humanistic idea of balance, born, so to speak, from the breath of the figures and from the need to put order, a rational order, into their actions. Even if Giotto did not know the mathematical rules of perspective, he expressed their moral essence, which is the attempt to bring human order into the universe.

It is interesting to note how this new sense of the world, which brings the painter within the threshold of the Renaissance, was still coupled with an absolutely mediaeval concept of abstraction. Stylization of form until line and volume become markedly geometrical, and the endeavour to simplify every motif by idealizing it within an elementary pattern, are characteristic of every hieratic form of expression which seeks to convey a sense of the perfection of the "divine" by means of an absolutely immobile geometrical system. Giotto's aim was to achieve this; he did not insist on the details of his figures or on a further development of the action, so as not to let the meaning fall to an episodic or casual level. He did not want to lose the force of mediaeval symbolism, or to deprive his stories of their supernatural character, which derived from their abstract formal purity. To this end he barely indicated the evolution of an action and was extremely restrained in his depiction of gestures, often preferring to indicate the most important things by the mere glances of the personages. Giotto's world is thus a world of potential rather than expressed actions, of internal rather than external movements, and though the gilded Byzantine background of the icons is no more, the blue of his skies is no less intact or less abstract. But it is precisely because of this that the human and the divine, the mediaeval and the Renaissance world could exist side by side, and none was better able than this master of the idea of heaven and earth to tell the story of the Christ who was God and man at the same time. The Padua frescoes mark not only the point at which there was perfect harmony in his life and art, but also the precious and unique moment when two cultures, directed toward such different ends, met.

Nobody knew how to render the profound meaning of a biblical story as well as he. The frescoes begin with Joachim driven out of the temple and taking refuge among shepherds. One of the first scenes represents Joachim's arrival in the mountains. In the Paduan frescoes the natural or architectural background is more than ever an integral part of the story. In "Joachim Taking Refuge among the Shepherds" (p. 32) the

17

fact that the foot of the mountain is on the side whence Joachim comes is enough to make us realize that he has just arrived and is about to begin his long stay as a hermit in the silence of the mountain country.

One of the scenes in which this allusive character of nature is most effective is "Joachim's Dream" (pp. 34, 35). Joachim is sleeping profoundly; the heaviness of the folds of his robe, which enclose the almost formless mass of his body, indicates the depth of his sleep, and the hut and the mountain rising behind him stress his isolation. A deep gulf of sky cuts him off from the shepherds, but it is from that gulf of the sky, which reaches down almost to Joachim's reclining head, that the angel's message comes, transmitted by the curving outline of the mountain which repeats its rhythm. In this indirect way the mysterious nature of this event and the transmission of the message to the sleeping figure are suggested.

The scene of the meeting of Joachim and Anne ("The Meeting at the Golden Gate") (pp. 36, 37) has the liveliness of a city street scene. The entrance arch, where a group of curious people stand, is like the threshold of a house. But the emotion of the meeting shows the solemnity of the event. The emotion is not so much in the affectionate embrace of Anne and Joachim as in the bending of the two bodies towards each other, in the harmony of their encounter and the peace achieved at the moment when they touch (p. 36).

One of the most audacious definitions of space is seen in the representation of the temple and the kneeling figures in the "Praying for the Rods to Flower" (p. 39), in which the convexity of the area filled with praying bodies is contrasted with the concavity of the hollow of the apse in a play of curved lines which might seem an end in itself, did not all that orderly gravity add an air of ceremony and expectancy.

Elsewhere it is the light itself on the colours which assumes

18   *(Continued on page 73)*

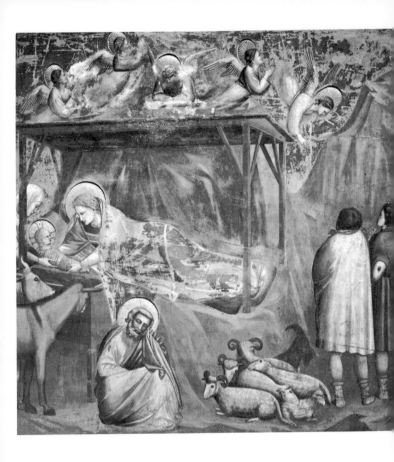

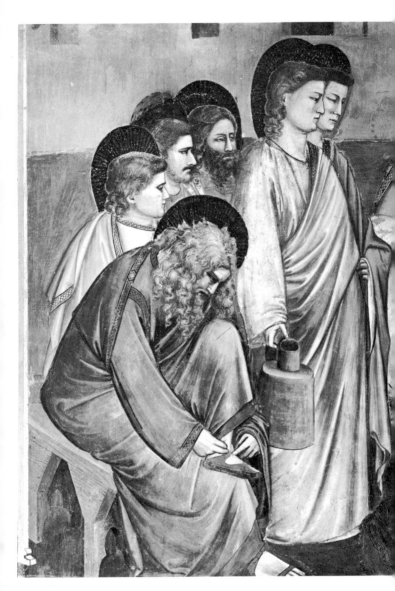

special significance, as in the "Annunciation to the Virgin" (p. 41), where the face of the Virgin is lit up in its submissive and conscious purity; her bosom seems to welcome the promise of motherhood.

"The Nativity" (p. 42) is set among lonely mountains. The poverty of the environment is indicated by the meagreness of the shed, and the solitude of the place by the curtain of mountains which almost fill the background and rise up to reach the angels whose rejoicing surprises the shepherds. The scene is dominated by the figure of the Virgin, which is gigantic, like a divinity in an ancient relief. In the great central space filled by her body, every other descriptive detail or narrative action is silenced.

In the following scene, the "Adoration of the Magi" (p. 43), Giotto is no longer concerned with stressing the wild loneliness of the country in which the miraculous event takes place; the mountains shrink near to the shed and fill a secondary position in order to make room for a lifelike ceremony which shows Joseph, Mary and the Child in an almost sorrowful attitude and soberly posed, while the Magi are elegantly described, with exotic touches.

One of the most intensely dramatic scenes is "The Flight into Egypt" (pp. 44, 45). Here the background with the repeated profiles of the two mountains has a double task. The repetition gives the feeling of a journey and changing scenery, and the monumentality of the nearer mountain provides a frame for the Virgin; Joseph and the other figures are absorbed into the incidental features of the journey; but the horizontal undulating rhythm in which the tale is unfolding in the foreground is broken abruptly in the middle by the long vertical line that runs from the top of the mountain down to the hem of the Virgin's mantle. The Virgin is defined by this line and given prominence by the frame of the mountain; she is isolated and imposes herself upon the scene through contrast. It has been observed that her eyes and thoughts are fixed beyond the events of the journey, that she is already fully conscious of the tragedy that awaits her.

There is a note of anguish in "The Slaughter of the Innocents" (pp. 46, 47). Giotto is a stranger to violence and rarely allows his drama to break out in disorderly tumult. When, as here, he wants to depict violence and brutality he is not afraid to use crude and vulgar forms. To his mind, evil is always associated with something deformed and dark; we find these features in "The Betrayal of Christ", in the "Christ before Caiaphas" and in "The Scourging of Christ", but above all in his description of hell. Conversely, the ideal of goodness is always accompanied by the ideal of beauty. This ideal was dear to ancient Greece, and Giotto's Christian conscience made it more profound.

The scene of "The Slaughter of the Innocents" is dominated by more angular, more broken forms, by tense and contrasting rhythms which give the sense of a desperate tragedy: the cruel gestures of the ruffians are opposed by the movements of the horrified mothers. The scene of "The Baptism of Christ" (pp. 48, 49) is dominated by an almost opposite emotion. Baptism means purification, and Giotto renders its essence by isolating Christ's body, detaching it from the surrounding mountains which open towards the sky. The naked, extremely sensitive body possesses a delicacy which seems to be striving to express all the human frailty of Jesus; it is immersed in water and in light; only the arm of the Baptist lightly touches it.

Worldly elements appear once again in "The Marriage at Cana" (p. 50), in the richness of the architecture, in the dignity of the personages, in the ostentatiousness of the large wine jars. But the feeling of the mystery of death and the tomb emerges in "The Raising of Lazarus" (p. 51), in which the immobile forms (the mountain, the embalmed body of Lazarus, the prostrate figures praying at Christ's feet) give a sense of petrified expect-ancy and are magnificently fused with other forms which move jerkily and create a feeling of anxiety and impatient desire for the miracle.

A wonderful rhythmic fluidity dominates "The Washing of the Feet" (pp. 52, 53), one of Giotto's most balanced compositions; he does not have to have recourse to mechanical symmetry, but simply makes use of rhythmic harmonies. The gestures of the figures, and the lines articulating their forms are ample and free; they fill space with movement and make you feel that this time Christ is not only pointing a moral but also setting a practical example.

In contrast with the orderly spontaneity of "The Washing of the Feet" is the artificial disorder of "The Betrayal of Christ" (p. 54). Here Christ's face emerging above Judas' mantle is like a rock beaten upon but unshaken by the violent gestures of the excited figures (p. 55).

To achieve the sense of tumult, the rhythms clash like the weapons pointed at different angles. But even here there is no confusion, and violence and force are expressed above all by the crowding forms closely massed together. And Giotto even succeeded in expressing the speed of events by repeating the same gestures. But the frenzy ceases around Christ's face, and the confrontation of the two faces, those of Christ and Judas, has the quality of eternity.

In the scene before Caiaphas (p. 57) the figure of Christ attains one of the sublimest expressions of composed dignity. It was enough for Giotto to turn Christ's face in a different direction from all the others to mark Him out and separate Him from the vulgar excitement of the scene. It has been said that His face expresses at the same time accusation and pardon, disdain and compassion (p. 56).

There follow the saddest scenes of the Passion. In "The Crucifixion" (pp. 58, 59) Giotto, who always used a vigorous plasticity, takes all bodily consistency away from Mary, in order to show the torment of her despair. But in "The Deposition" (p. 60) the anguish of the figure in the foreground has the immobility of a person turned to stone by sorrow. The main lines of the composition direct the attention towards the Mother's look of anguish as she supports her Son's head. The lines fall inertly like a rain of tears, and the sky above the scene, though vast, is filled with grievously agitated angels.

An equally vast sky dominates the scene of the "Noli Me Tangere" (p. 61). It stretches from the mountain which contains the tomb as far as the figure of Christ as if to indicate His divine destiny. Christ is walking towards the light, towards freedom; he is leaving the world, and the tall standard, waving in the wind, at the extreme edge of the picture indicates the life pervading that great sky, the sky of the Resurrection. Nor is this the only sign by which we are to understand the miracle of the renewal of life. As the mute dialogue between the hands of Christ and the hands of the Magdalen takes place, verdant plants spring up on the bare mountain, bursting with physical vitality. "Noli me tangere" means "Do not touch me", and the hands seek each other without touching, but communicate the accord between the ecstatic emotion of the Magdalen and the peace of Christ.

The huge subject of "The Last Judgement" (p. 62) involved Giotto in a composition which is still closely linked with mediaeval symbolism. But although in many ways symbolism prevails, we see in the details solutions of proportioned and coherent space, as in the episode of Enrico Scrovegni donating the chapel (p. 63). The iconographic and liturgical order of the Saints and the Blessed is contrasted to the disorder of the damned. At one time critics were inclined to see the work of collaborators in many of these scenes, and especially in the

Judgement, but now it is generally held that almost all the decorations of the chapel are by Giotto; nearly all the paintings representing the Vices and Virtues which decorate the socles (bases) of the walls are also ascribed to him. The monochrome in which these figures (p. 64) are painted is well adapted to his plasticism; but their most interesting feature is the artist's interpretation of moral attitudes, the essence of which he personifies with a rare force of characterization, using every descriptive detail for his purpose.

The 'Ognissanti Madonna" (pp. 65, 66) in the Uffizi in Florence may be placed chronologically very near to the Paduan frescoes. The gigantic Madonna is seated on a throne the refinement and richness of which are described in the Gothic manner. In accordance with the iconography of the time, the Virgin is portrayed as of superhuman size, because the devout eye saw her as gigantic. It is impossible to understand her unless we think of her faithful worshippers who wanted her to be as large as the extent of their enthusiasm and love. Angels and saints are arranged about her in a symmetry that is still liturgical, but even in their orderly silence a separate individuality is revealed in each of them. Giotto was no longer thinking in terms of anonymous symbols, but always in terms of human characterization.

The painted crucifix at Rimini (p. 67) dates from not much later than the frescoes of Padua (some critics doubt its authenticity). It is surrounded by hieratically precious and extremely refined decoration, but it is also solemn and full of anguish and drama, these qualities being expressed by the large body, the wide open arms, the deeply emotional and sensitive rendering of every detail, as if the devout brush hardly dared to delineate the figure.

It would take too much space to discuss all the works which came after the Padua frescoes, but one of them, "The Dormition of the Virgin", at Berlin, should at least be mentioned as an outstanding work.

We have more numerous documents for the last period of Giotto's life, which show that he lived for a time at Rome, Milan, Naples and Florence, where he died in 1337, having begun — and also, probably, designed the decorations for — a notable work of architecture, the campanile of the Church of Santa Maria del Fiore. But the major works which remain from this period are the frescoes of the Bardi and Peruzzi chapels in the Church of Santa Croce in Florence, where he had already painted two other chapels. These frescoes are difficult to date; it is only a supposition that the Peruzzi Chapel was painted after 1320 and the Bardi Chapel after 1325.

The frescoes in Santa Croce at Florence are in various states of preservation. Repainting in the Peruzzi Chapel has made it impossible to restore the originals; therefore, only the main lines of the compositions can have any valid significance for us. But in the Bardi Chapel, in spite of the missing parts, we can still admire Giotto's art in its last phase.

A feature shared by both cycles is a new feeling for space. Giotto has enlarged his vision; his scenes are now broader and deeper, the relation between figures and architecture more naturalistically proportioned than in Padua. He has taken a further step towards the Renaissance by pushing back the closed background of his scenes; his figures now have more room for their actions, but he is not, therefore, less logical or well balanced. More figures now take part in his scenes, and the story is less concentrated on one event, and dissolves more easily into a greater number of episodes. This less epic and more narrative tendency makes possible a greater development of the dialogue between the characters. At Padua and at Assisi there was a clear distinction between the principal figures and the minor actors; here the distance between the dominant figure and the subordinate ones is less evident. In fact, a less authoritarian and more democratic, a less theological and more worldly society now begins to appear in Giotto's art. Because of this, what was lost in the power of the whole was compensated for by variety and movement, so that, all in all, the last phase of Giotto's art was not less lofty than the earlier phases. His buildings, also, of which those in "The Raising of Drusiana" (p. 68) are typical, are not only larger, but more complex, and the story tends to centre about more focal points.

A comparison between "The Deposition" at Padua (p. 60) and "The Death of St. Francis" (p. 71) in the Bardi Chapel shows us that in the former everything converges towards the heads of the Virgin and Christ, but it could not be said that the area around the Saint in the latter picture dominates the rest in such an absolute manner. The rhythmical wave which guides the composition is stopped several times in its course around the body of the Saint by the testimonies of affection expressed by the kneeling friars (pp. 70, 71 and 72).

But the novelty of the later Giotto lies not only in his new mode of composition, but also in his new use of colour. Naturally, these changes have very complex roots; in part, they result from the development of certain experiments made before Giotto's time and the changes occurring in his entire culture. The Gothic tide was surging around Giotto, giving life to the impulse towards naturalistic interests, towards complex composition and, above all, under the influence of the neighbouring Sienese art, towards richer and more subtle colouring. But Giotto did not only add new interests to the older ones; for example, he did not abandon his spacious monumentality to the enchantments of charmingly coloured surfaces; from the new culture he took only what served to enrich certain aspects of his traditional style. What Giotto developed during this last phase of his painting was, above all, the emo-

79

tional element in his narratives. It could be said that he abandoned the epic and turned to elegy. His descriptions became particularly mild, gentle and full of sweetness. He expressed this new language through colour — by using the lightest shades, the freshest surfaces, the most delicate passages set between lines that had become less decisive. An affectionate tenderness veiled the eyes of the aging Giotto, and in this intimate and moving way the most truly Franciscan of painters came to his end.

We began with St. Francis, and to St. Francis we must return to conclude. Perhaps there has never been any artist in whom moral problems were so intensely lived as in Giotto, and this links him with the other great figure who dominated the Italian culture of the time, with Dante.

Giotto and Dante, so different in character and in the vicissitudes of their lives, were nevertheless very near to each other in their striving to confront the human conscience with the world, in their attempt to break away from the Middle Ages, of which they were both children; they were the first to unite those various currents of Italian culture which were to determine its character forever.

LIST OF ILLUSTRATIONS

The illustrations on pages 19 and 21-31 show frescoes in the Church of St. Francis, Assisi, of about 1296-99.

The illustrations on pages 32-64 show frescoes in the Scrovegni Chapel (Arena Chapel), Padua, of about 1305.

67 CRUCIFIX
About 1306; panel; 169¼ × 119¼ in.
Malatestiano Temple, Rimini

68 THE RAISING OF DRUSIANA
About 1320; fresco; 110¼ × 119¼ in.
Peruzzi Chapel, Church of Sta. Croce, Florence

The illustrations on pages 69-72 show frescoes in the Bardi Chapel, Church of Sta. Croce, Florence (of about 1325).

69 THE APPARITION TO BROTHER AUGUSTINE
Detail of the friars

70 THE DEATH OF ST. FRANCIS
Detail of friars

71 THE DEATH OF ST. FRANCIS
110¼ × 177⅛ in.

72 THE DEATH OF ST. FRANCIS
Detail of friar kissing the hand of St. Francis